Declaration of Independence

Written by Douglas M. Rife
Illustrated by Bron Smith

Teaching & Learning Company
1204 Buchanan St., P.O. Box 10
Carthage, IL 62321-0010

This book belongs to

_____

Cover: John Trumbull
The Declaration of Independence, 4 July 1776 (detail)
Yale University Art Gallery
Trumbull Collection

Copyright © 1997, Teaching & Learning Company

ISBN No. 1-57310-077-3

Printing No. 987654

Teaching & Learning Company
1204 Buchanan St., P.O. Box 10
Carthage, IL 62321-0010

ii

Table of Contents

Dear Teacher or Parent,

The Declaration of Independence is arguably the most important document in American history, for without it there would be no American history at all. It is the founding document of our nation. It is on its passage that we celebrate the birth of our nation. It is the document with which our nation asserted many of the basic principals that still govern our legislative efforts and our individual consciousnesses.

The study of the Declaration of Independence is a good way to introduce young history students to primary source documents. This reproducible book provides activities for students to investigate the Declaration of Independence, as well as place it in the larger context of events that led to its creation.

Sincerely,

Douglas M. Rife

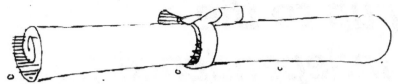

Objectives

After completing the following activities	the students should be able to . . .
Events Leading up to the Declaration of Independence	1. identify major events leading up to the revolution 2. place historical events in a time line 3. define reasons the colonials wanted independence
Boston Massacre	1. understand the events leading up to the massacre 2. contrast what happened in the Revere depiction 3. identify loaded words 4. view art critically
Signers of the Declaration of Independence	1. understand who the signers were 2. extrapolate information from a chart 3. draw conclusions from data 4. design bar and pie graphs
Understanding the Declaration	1. put the Declaration in an historic perspective 2. synthesize parts of the Declaration and restate it in their own words 3. explain the reasons that the Continental Congress listed to declare independence
Franklin's Cartoons	1. identify the parts of Franklin's cartoon 2. interpret the political message 3. draw own cartoons

Events Leading up to the Declaration of Independence

1760 October 26, following the death of King George II, his grandson, George III ascends to the British throne.

1764 April 5, Parliament passes the *Sugar Act*. The Sugar Act raises taxes on items being shipped into the American colonies such as sugar, wine, coffee, dyes and cloth. The act reduces taxes on molasses from the French Caribbean. The colonies protest.

April 19, Parliament passes the *Currency Act* prohibiting the colonies from issuing paper money. Because silver and gold are not permitted to be imported into the colonies, it is difficult to conduct business.

1765 March 22, the *Stamp Act* becomes law. The Stamp Act imposes a tax on most paper goods—playing cards, newspapers, books, pamphlets—and all legal documents registered are taxed as well, such as wills, deeds and tax documents. Opposition to the Stamp Act is formed quickly. Open demonstrations take place. Protest groups form. Tax collectors are harassed and threatened. The Sons of Liberty organize to resist and to gain repeal of the Stamp Act.

May 15, Parliament passes the *Quartering Act* which orders the colonists to provide British troops a place to live and to provide them with certain provisions such as salt, blankets and candles.

October 7, the Stamp Act Congress meets. Delegates from Massachusetts, Connecticut, Rhode Island, New Jersey, South Carolina, Delaware, Maryland, Pennsylvania and New York meet in New York to protest the Stamp Act and "taxation without representation." The delegates craft a declaration of rights and grievances. The Stamp Act Congress adjourns October 25.

1766 March 18, under pressure from British merchants suffering from a depression and the colonial boycott of British goods, Parliament repeals the Stamp Act on the same day it passed the *Declaratory Act*. The Declaratory Act reaffirmed Parliament's right to legislate for the colonies "in all cases whatsoever."

1767   June-July, Parliament passes the *Townshend Acts*. The acts, the *Revenue Act* taxes glass, lead, tea, paper and painters' colors imported into the colonies and the *New York Restraining Act* suspends the New York legislature until the colony supplies and houses the British soldiers stationed there under the provisions of the Quartering Act. The troops are to be fed and housed in private homes, warehouses and public buildings. The Townshend Acts also establish a custom board of commissioners to be located in Boston to collect taxes and supervise trade. The customs officials in turn appoint deputies. All of these officials are paid from the taxes collected from the colonials.

1768   October 1, British soldiers arrive in Boston to enforce customs laws.

1769   Parliament passes a resolution allowing colonials accused of treason to be sent to Britain for trial.

1770   March 5, Boston Massacre occurs, five colonists killed by British troops.

April 12, except for the tax on tea, Parliament repeals the Townshend Revenue Acts.

1772   November 2, Samuel Adams and Joseph Warren of Massachusetts organize committees of correspondence.

1773   December 16, men disguised as Mohawks throw the tea on board three docked ships into Boston Harbor. This becomes known as the Boston Tea Party.

1774   May 13, General Gage arrives in Boston to command British troops stationed there.

May 20, the King gives his assent to the first two of four acts known as the *Coercive Acts*. The *Impartial Administration of Justice Act* gave the governor the power to move trials from Massachusetts to other colonies and to England. The *Massachusetts Government Act* virtually took all control of the colony from the legislative assembly to the royal governor. The act provided that all officers of the law be appointed by the governor and all town meetings be suspended without approval of the governor. Under this act, General Gage is appointed governor of Massachusetts.

March 31, the *Boston Port Act* moved the capital to Salem and established Marblehead as the port of entry. It also provided that the port of Boston would remain closed until the tea that had been dumped at the Boston Tea Party was paid for.

June 2, the *Quartering Act* passed by Parliament mandated that the colonists house and feed the British soldiers stationed in Massachusetts.

June 22, the *Quebec Act* passes Parliament granting Quebec large grants of land that the American colonists considered theirs for settlement.

September 1, Massachusetts's stock of powder at Charlestown is seized by General Gage and the British troops.

September 5, representatives from 12 of the colonies assembled in Carpenter's Hall in Philadelphia and organized the first Continental Congress. Only Georgia was not represented.

October 14, the Declaration of Rights and Grievances is adopted by Congress.

October 26, the First Continental Congress adjourns.

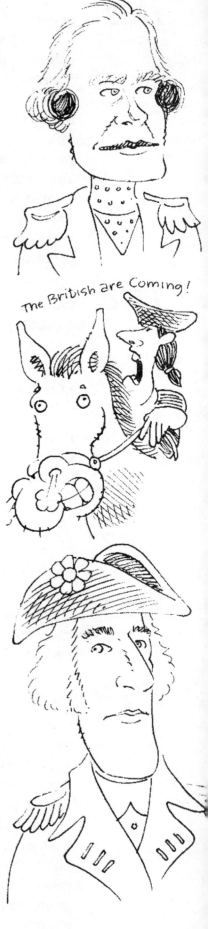

The British are Coming!

1775

March 30, the *New York Restraining Act* restricted trade between the colonies and any countries except England. The act also limited fishing rights in the North Atlantic.

April 18/19, Paul Revere and William Dawes take midnight ride to warn that the British are advancing. Revere is captured by the British and released the next morning.

April 19, the battles of Lexington and Concord take place. The first shots of the war were fired at the Battle of Lexington.

May 10, all 13 colonies send delegates to Philadelphia to the Second Continental Congress. The Congress meets at the Pennsylvania State House (which later becomes known as Independence Hall).

June 15, the Continental Congress appoints George Washington Commander of the Continental Army.

June 17, British victory at the battle of Bunker Hill (over 1,000 troops killed or wounded; more than 400 colonists killed or wounded).

July 8, Congress adopts a petition offering reconcilation to be sent to the king.

September 1, the congressional July 8 petition to the king is refused.

1776 January 9, Thomas Paine's fiery pamphlet, *Common Sense*, is published. In just a few short months over 150,000 copies sell throughout the colonies.

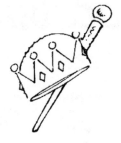

1776 Declaration of Independence

June 7, Richard Henry Lee, chairman of the Virginia delegation, offers a resolution in Congress: "That these United Colonies are, and of right ought to be, free and independent States, that they are absolved from all allegiance to the British Crown, and that all political connection between them and the State of Great Britain is, and ought to be, totally dissolved." John Adams seconded the motion.

June 11, a committee of five is appointed by the Continental Congress to draft a Declaration of Independence. Benjamin Franklin, Roger Sherman, John Adams, Robert Livingston and Thomas Jefferson are appointed to the committee to write the Declaration of Independence. Adams wrote that Jefferson "brought with him a reputation for literature, science, and a happy talent for composition. Writings of his were handed about remarkable for the peculiar felicity of expression. Though a silent member in Congress, he was so prompt, frank, explicit, and decisive upon committees and in conversation."

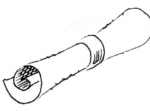

July 2, Lee's June 7th resolution is adopted by Congress.

July 4, the Declaration of Independence, as amended, is adopted by Congress. President of Congress, John Hancock and secretary Charles Thompson sign it.

July 9, Congress orders the Declaration of Independence be engrossed on parchment suitable for signing.

August 2, the Declaration of Independence is signed by the 50 members of Congress present. After hearing someone comment that all signers "must hang together," Benjamin Franklin remarks, "Yes, we must all hang together or we shall hang separately."

August 27, George Wythe signs the Declaration.

September, Richard Henry Lee, Elbridge Gerry and Oliver Wolcott sign the Declaration.

November, Matthew Thornton signs the Declaration.

1781 Sometime during this year, Colonel Thomas McKean signs the Declaration of Independence. Though present during the voting, he had been absent on August 2, 1776, when most members of Congress signed the parchment. McKean is the last person to sign the document.

Vocabulary Match

Write the letter of the correct definition in the blank next to each word.

_____ 1. prohibit

_____ 2. import

_____ 3. impose

_____ 4. harass

_____ 5. repeal

_____ 6. quarter

_____ 7. grievance

_____ 8. customs

_____ 9. assent

_____ 10. coerce

_____ 11. mandate

_____ 12. reconciliation

_____ 13. allegiance

_____ 14. felicity

A. to bring about by force

B. a settlement, restoration of friendship

C. a duty or tax on imported goods

D. loyalty or obedience

E. to establish by authority

F. to withdraw by authoritative act

G. expression of agreement

H. a pleasing quality (especially in language)

I. to provide with lodging or shelter

J. an authoritative command

K. to bring into

L. to prevent from doing something

M. complaint or protest

N. to annoy repeatedly

Handout 2

Name _____

Independence Scramble

Answer each statement below with words that fit in the spaces exactly. When you are finished, unscramble the letters in the circles of the first nine to answer #10.

1. He was the author of the Declaration of Independence.

   __ __ __ __ __ __ __   __ __ __ Ⓞ __ __ __ __ __

2. He was the ruler of England during the American Revolution.

   __ __ __ __ __   __ __ __ __ __ Ⓞ __   __ __ __ __

3. Because of this, British soldiers were housed in colonials' homes.

   __ __ __ __ __ Ⓞ __ __ __ __ __   __ __ __ __

4. This body met in Philadelphia and voted on the Declaration of Independence.

   Ⓞ __ __ __ __ __ Ⓞ __ __ __ __   __ __ __ __ __ __ __ __

5. He was one of the organizers of the committees of correspondence.

   __ __ __ __ __ __ __   Ⓞ __ __ __

6. He commanded the Continental Army.

   __ Ⓞ __ __ __ __   __ __ __ __ __ __ __ __ Ⓞ

7. He proposed the resolution in Congress, June 7, 1775, "that these United Colonies are, and of right ought to be free, . . ."

   __ __ __ __ __ __ Ⓞ __   __ __ __ __ __   __ __ __

8. The first shots of the war were here.

   __ __ __ __ __ __ __ Ⓞ __

9. This is the representative body of England.

   Ⓞ __ __ Ⓞ __ __ __ __ __

10. The representatives to the Second Continental Congress voted for this on July 4, 1776.

    __ __ __ __ __ __ __ __ __ __ __

Name _____

Act on It—Matching

Write the letter identifying the act passed by Parliament next to the numeral that best describes it.

_____ 1. Gave the Massachusetts govenor power to relocate trials.

_____ 2. This act raised taxes on items being shipped into the colonies such as wine, coffee, dyes, cloth and sugar.

_____ 3. This act prohibited the colonies from printing money.

_____ 4. This act taxed most paper goods—newspapers, playing cards, books, pamphlets and all legal documents.

_____ 5. Taxed imported glass, tea, lead and painters' colors.

_____ 6. This act closed the Port of Boston.

_____ 7. This kind of act was passed in 1765 and 1774 and mandated that the colonists house and feed British soldiers.

_____ 8. Established a customs board commissioner to collect taxes.

_____ 9. Parliament states that it has authority over the colonies "in all cases whatsoever."

_____ 10. Consisted of four acts—aimed at Massachusetts in part for the Boston Tea Party.

A. Quartering Act

B. Sugar Act

C. Stamp Act

D. Currency Act

E. Declaratory Act

F. Boston Port Act

G. Revenue Act

H. Impartial Administration of Justice Act

I. Coercive Acts

J. Townshend Acts

Handout 4

Revolutionary Time Line

Look at the list of events below. Then write the event next to the year that it took place.

Declaration of Independence signed
George III becomes king
Battle of Lexington
Stamp Act
Sugar Act

Boston Tea Party
Revenue Act
First Continental Congress meets
Boston Massacre

1760– _____

1764– _____

1765– _____

1767– _____

1770– _____

1773– _____

1774– _____

1775– _____

1776– _____

Boston Massacre

On March 5, Edward Gerrish, a young apprentice, hurled insults at a British soldier, standing in the square by the Boston Customs House. Private Hugh White, a British soldier posted at the Customs House, hit Gerrish from behind. A crowd began to form. Private White held his ground with his bayonet fixed, the other soldier left. The crowd turned into a mob. The mob taunted and pelted White with ice and snowballs. Captain Thomas Preston, from a nearby British guard post marched seven soldiers, a corporal and six privates, to the Customs House to restore order. The soldiers fixed their bayonets and formed a line in front of the Customs House. There was a great deal of confusion and the events that followed are unclear. Someone threw ice and a soldier slipped. While regaining his footing, the soldier's gun discharged—the other soldiers took aim at the angry mob and fired. Three men in the mob were killed instantly, another man died within hours and another died a few days later.

Carefully look at Paul Revere's engraving and answer the questions below.
1. According to the account of the massacre given in the handout, who is the soldier with his sword risen?
2. How many British soldiers has Revere pictured in the engraving?
3. Why would Revere use the term *Butcher's Hall*?

Questions for Further Discussion

1. A trial took place. The British soldiers were tried for murder, defended by attorneys John Adams and Josiah Quincy. Do you think the soldiers were found guilty or not guilty?
2. Loaded words are words that are emotionally charged. Which words in the title above Revere's engraving are loaded? Why would Revere use loaded words?
3. Does Revere depict a point of view that is favorable to the British soldiers or to the colonists? Why?
4. If a British artist illustrated the Boston Massacre, how might it look different?

Boston Massacre

Shortly after the Boston Massacre, Paul Revere sold copies of the engraving below. Above the engraving read the following title:

"THE FRUITS OF ARBITRARY POWER, OR THE BLOODY MASSACRE, PERPETRATED IN KING STREET BOSTON MARCH 5, 1770, IN WHICH MESS.RS SAML GRAY, SAML MAVERICK, JAMES CALDWELL, CRISPUS ATTUCKS, PATRICK CARR WERE KILLED, SIX OTHER WOUNDED TWO OF THEM MORTALLY."

Signers of the Declaration of Independence

State Represented Signer Birth-Death Dates	Occupation	Religion	National Origin	Age at Signing
Massachusetts				
Samuel Adams (Sept. 27, 1722-Oct. 2, 1803)	Politician	Congregational	English	53
John Hancock (Jan. 23, 1737-Oct. 8, 1793)	Merchant	Congregational	English	39
John Adams (Oct. 19, 1735-July 4, 1826)	Lawyer	Unitarian	English	40
Elbridge Gerry (July 17, 1744-Nov. 23, 1814)	Merchant	Episcopal	English	31
Robert Treat Paine (Mar. 11, 1731-May 11, 1814)	Lawyer	Unitarian	English	45
Virginia				
Thomas Jefferson (Apr. 13, 1743-July 4, 1826)	Planter	Unitarian	English	33
Richard Henry Lee (Jan. 20, 1732-June 19, 1794)	Planter	Episcopal	English	44
Benjamin Harrison (1726-Apr. 24, 1791)	Planter	Episcopal	English	50
Francis Lightfoot Lee (Oct. 14, 1743-Jan. 11, 1797)	Planter	Episcopal	English	41
Thomas Nelson, Jr. (Dec. 26, 1738-Jan. 4, 1789)	Planter	Episcopal	Scottish-English	31
George Wythe (1726-June 8, 1806)	Lawyer	Episcopal	English	50
Carter Braxton (Sept. 10, 1736-Oct. 10, 1797)	Planter	Episcopal	English	39
Pennsylvania				
Benjamin Franklin (Jan. 17, 1706-Apr. 17, 1790)	Printer	Diest	English	70
Robert Morris (Jan. 31, 1734-May 8, 1806)	Merchant	Episcopal	English	42
Benjamin Rush (Jan. 4, 1746-Apr. 19, 1813)	Physician	Episcopal, Presbyterian	English	30
John Morton (1724-Apr. 1777)	Farmer	Episcopal	Swedish-English	52
George Clymer (Mar. 16, 1739-Jan. 24, 1813)	Merchant	Episcopal	English	37
James Smith (1719-July 11, 1806)	Lawyer	Presbyterian, Episcopal	Scotch-Irish	37
George Taylor (1716-Feb. 23, 1781)	Ironmaster	Episcopal	Scotch-Irish	60
James Wilson (Sept. 14, 1742-Aug. 21, 1798)	Lawyer	Presbyterian	Scottish	33
George Ross (May 10, 1730-July 14, 1779)	Lawyer	Episcopal	Scottish	49

State Represented Signer Birth-Death Dates	Occupation	Religion	National Origin	Age at Signing
New Jersey				
John Witherspoon (Feb. 5, 1723-Nov. 15, 1794)	Clergyman	Presbyterian	Scottish	53
Richard Stockton (Oct. 1, 1730-Feb. 28, 1781)	Lawyer	Presbyterian	English	45
Francis Hopkinson (Oct. 2, 1737-May 9, 1791)	Lawyer	Episcopal	English	38
John Hart (1711-May 11, 1779)	Farmer	Baptist	English	65
Abraham Clark (Feb. 15, 1726-Sept. 15, 1794)	Surveyor	Presbyterian	English	50
New York				
Philip Livingston (Jan. 15, 1716-June 12, 1778)	Merchant	Presbyterian	Dutch-Scottish	60
Lewis Morris (Apr. 8, 1726-Jan. 22, 1798)	Landowner	Episcopal	Dutch-Scottish	50
William Floyd (Dec. 17, 1734-Aug. 4, 1821)	Landowner	Presbyterian	Welsh-English	41
Francis Lewis (Mar. 21, 1713-Dec. 31, 1802)	Merchant	Episcopal	Welsh	63
Connecticut				
Roger Sherman (Apr. 30, 1721-July 23, 1793)	Lawyer	Congregational	English	55
Samuel Huntington (July 3, 1731-Jan. 5, 1796)	Lawyer	Congregational	English	45
William Williams (Apr. 8, 1731-Aug. 2, 1811)	Merchant	Congregational	English	45
Oliver Wolcott (Nov. 20, 1726-Dec. 1, 1797)	Lawyer	Congregational	English	49
Rhode Island				
Stephen Hopkins (Mar. 7, 1707-July 13, 1785)	Merchant	Quaker	English	69
William Ellery (Dec. 22, 1727-Feb. 15, 1820)	Lawyer	Congregational	English	48
New Hampshire				
Josiah Bartlett (Nov. 21, 1729-May 19, 1795)	Judge	Congregational	English	46
William Whipple (Jan. 14, 1730-Nov. 10, 1785)	Merchant	Congregational	English	46
Matthew Thornton (1714-June 24, 1803)	Physician	Congregational	Scotch-Irish	62

State Represented Signer Birth-Death Dates	Occupation	Religion	National Origin	Age at Signing
Maryland				
Charles Carroll of Carrollton (Sept. 19, 1737-Nov. 14, 1832)	Planter	Roman Catholic	Irish	38
Thomas Stone (1734-Oct. 5, 1787)	Lawyer	Episcopal	English	33
William Paca (Oct. 31, 1740-Oct. 13, 1799)	Lawyer	Episcopal	Italian-English	35
Samuel Chase (Apr. 17, 1741-June 19, 1811)	Lawyer	Espiscopal	English	35
Delaware				
Caesar Rodney (Oct. 7, 1728-June 26, 1784)	Planter	Episcopal	English	47
Thomas McKean (Mar. 19, 1734-June 24, 1817)	Lawyer	Presbyterian	Scotch-Irish	42
George Read (Sept. 18, 1733-Sept. 21, 1798)	Lawyer	Episcopal	Irish-Welsh	42
North Carolina				
William Hooper (June 17, 1742-Oct. 14, 1790)	Lawyer	Congregational	English	34
Joseph Hewes (Jan. 23, 1730-Nov. 10, 1779)	Merchant	Episcopal	English	46
John Penn (May 6, 1740-Sept. 14, 1788)	Lawyer	Episcopal	English	36
South Carolina				
Thomas Heyward, Jr. (July 28, 1746-Mar. 6, 1809)	Lawyer	Episcopal	English	30
Arthur Middleton (June 26, 1742-Jan. 1, 1787)	Planter	Episcopal	English	34
Edward Rutledge (Nov. 23, 1749-Jan. 23, 1800)	Planter	Episcopal	English	26
Thomas Lynch, Jr. (Aug. 5, 1749-1779)	Lawyer	Episcopal	Irish-Dutch-English	26
Georgia				
Lyman Hall (Apr. 12, 1724-Oct. 19, 1790)	Physician	Congregational	English	52
Button Gwinnett (Apr. 1735-May 16, 1777)	Physician	Congregational	English	41
George Walton (1741-Feb. 2, 1804)	Lawyer	Episcopal	English	35

Note: Most of the signers had several careers in their lifetimes. Only the occupations that dominated their lives are listed.

Name _____

Who Were They?

Use Handout 8 (pages 16-18) about the signers to answer the following questions:

1. How many men signed the Declaration of Independence?_____

2. What was the average age of the signers? _____

3. Who was the oldest signer?_____

4. Who was the youngest signer? _____

5. What was the national origin of most of the delegates? _____

6. What percent of the delegates were English? _____
Make a pie graph showing the delegates' national orgins by percent.

7. What was the most common occupation of the delegates? _____
Make a pie graph showing the delegates' occupations by percent.

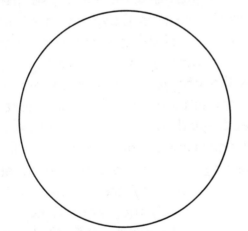

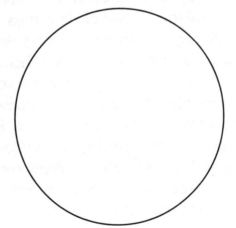

Questions for Further Discussion

1. Why were the signers all men? _____

2. Why were women not represented at the Congress? _____

_____

Declaration of Independence

Text of the Declaration

IN CONGRESS, JULY 4, 1776.

The unanimous Declaration of the thirteen united States of America,

When in the Course of human events, it becomes necessary for one people to dissolve the political bands which have connected them with another, and to assume among the powers of the earth, the separate and equal station to which the Laws of Nature and of Nature's God entitle them, a decent respect to the opinions of mankind requires that they should declare the causes which impel them to the separation.

We hold these truths to be self-evident, that all men are created equal, that they are endowed by their Creator with certain unalienable Rights, that among these are Life, Liberty and the pursuit of Happiness.—That to secure these rights, Governments are instituted among Men, deriving their powers from the consent of the governed.—That whenever any Form of Government becomes destructive of these ends, it is the Right of the People to alter or to abolish it, and to institute new Government, laying its foundation on such principles and organizing its powers in such form, as to them shall seem most likely to effect their Safety and Happiness. Prudence, indeed, will dictate that Governments long established should not be changed for light and transient causes; and accordingly all experience hath shewn, that mankind are more disposed to suffer, while evils are sufferable, than to right themselves by abolishing the forms to which they are accustomed. But when a long train of abuses and usurpations, pursuing invariably the same Object evinces a design to reduce them under absolute Despotism, it is their right, it is their duty, to throw off such Government, and to provide new Guards for their future security.—Such has been the patient sufferance of these Colonies; and such is now the necessity which constrains them to alter their future Systems of Government. The history of the present King of Great Britain is a history of repeated injuries and usurpations, all having in direct object the establishment of an absolute Tyranny over these States. To prove this, let Facts be submitted to a candid world.

He has refused his Assent to Laws, the most wholesome and necessary for the public good.

He has forbidden his Governors to pass Laws of immediate and pressing importance, unless suspended in their operation till his Assent should be obtained; and when so suspended, he has utterly neglected to attend to them.

He has refused to pass other Laws for the accommodation of large districts of people, unless those people would relinquish the right of Representation in the Legislature, a right inestimable to them and formidable to tyrants only.

He has called together legislative bodies at places unusual, uncomfortable, and distant from the depository of their public Records, for the sole purpose of fatiguing them into compliance with his measures.

He has dissolved Representative Houses repeatedly, for opposing with manly firmness his invasions on the rights of the people.

He has refused for a long time, after such dissolutions, to cause others to be elected; whereby the Legislative powers, incapable of Annihilation, have returned to the People at large for their exercise; the State remaining in the meantime exposed to all the dangers of invasion from without, and convulsions within.

He has endeavoured to prevent the population of these States; for that purpose obstructing the Laws for Naturalization of Foreigners; refusing to pass others to encourage their migrations hither, and raising the conditions of new Appropriations of Lands.

He has obstructed the Administration of Justice, by refusing his Assent to Laws for establishing Judiciary powers.

He has made Judges dependent on his Will alone, for the tenure of their offices, and the amount of payment of their salaries.

He has erected a multitude of New Offices, and sent hither swarms of Officers to harass our people, and eat out their substance.

He has kept among us, in times of peace, standing Armies without the Consent of our legislatures.

He has affected to render the Military independent of and superior to the Civil power.

He has combined with others to subject us to a jurisdiction foreign to our constitution, and unacknowledged by our laws; giving his Assent to their Acts of pretended Legislation:

For quartering large bodies of armed troops among us:

For protecting them, by a mock Trial, from punishment for any Murders which they should commit on the Inhabitants of the States:

For cutting off our Trade with all parts of the world:

For imposing Taxes on us without our Consent:

For depriving us in many cases, of the benefits of Trial by Jury:

For transporting us beyond Seas to be tried for pretended offences:

For abolishing the free System of English Laws in neighbouring Province, establishing therein an Arbitrary government, and enlarging its Boundaries so as to render it at once an example and fit instrument for introducing the same absolute rule into these Colonies:

For taking away our Charters, abolishing our most valuable Laws, and altering fundamentally the Forms of our Governments:

For suspending our own Legislatures and declaring themselves invested with power to legislate for us in all cases whatsoever.

He has abdicated Government here, by declaring us out of his Protection and waging War against us.

He has plundered our seas, ravaged our Coasts, burnt our towns, and destroyed the lives of our people.

He is at this time transporting large Armies of foreign Mercenaries to compleat the works of death, desolation and tyranny, already begun with circumstances of Cruelty & perfidy scarcely paralleled in the most barbarous ages, and totally unworthy the Head of a civilized nation.

He has constrained our fellow Citizens taken Captive on the high Seas to bear Arms against their Country, to become the executioners of their friends and Brethren, or to fall themselves by their Hands.

He has excited domestic insurrections amongst us, and has endeavoured to bring on the inhabitants of our frontiers, the merciless Indian Savages, whose known rule of warfare, is an undistinguished destruction of all ages, sexes and conditions.

In every stage of these Oppressions we have Petitioned for Redress in the most humble terms: our repeated Petitions have been answered only by repeated injury. A Prince, whose character is thus remarked by every act which may define a Tyrant, is unfit to be ruler of a free people.

Nor have we been wanting in attention to our British brethren. We have warned them from time to time of attempts by their legislature to extend an unwarrantable jurisdiction over us. We have reminded them of the circumstances of our emigration and settlement here. We have Appealed to their native justice and magnanimity, and we have conjured them by the ties of our common kindred to disavow these usurpations, which, would inevitably interrupt our connections and correspondence. They too have been deaf to the voice of justice and consanguinity. We must, therefore, acquiesce in the necessity, which denounces our Separation, and hold them, as we hold the rest of mankind, Enemies in War, in Peace Friends.

We, therefore, the Representatives of the united States of America, in General Congress, Assembled, appealing to the Supreme Judge of the world for the rectitude of our intentions, do in the Name, and by Authority of the good people of these Colonies, solemnly publish and declare, That these United Colonies are, and of Right ought to be Free and Independent States; that they are Absolved from all Allegiance of the British Crown, and that all political connection between them and the State of Great Britain, is and ought to be totally dissolved; and that as Free and Independent States, they have full Power to levy War, conclude Peace, contract Alliances, establish Commerce, and to do all other Acts and Things which Independent States may of right do.

And for the support of this Declaration, with a firm reliance on the protection of divine Providence, we mutually pledge to each other our Lives, our Fortunes and our sacred Honor.

Name _____

Understanding the Declaration of Independence

A.

Carefully read the Declaration of Independence and answer the following questions. (If necessary, use other resources.)

1. According to the authors, what is the purpose of paragraph 1? _____

_____

_____

2. What are the *unalienable* rights found in paragraph 2? _____

_____

_____

3. Who bestows unalienable rights? _____

4. According to the authors of the Declaration of Independence, from what source does

government get its power to govern? _____

_____

_____

5. When can the governed form a new government? _____

_____

_____

6. How is government like a contract between two people? _____

_____

_____

7. Why would the Continental Congress want to submit the "facts to a candid world"?

_____

_____

Name _____

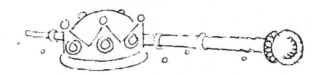

B. Grievances

Read the following grievances listed, then match them to the actions taken by the king or Parliament. Which actions match which grievances?

_____ 1. He has refused his Assent to Laws, the most necessary for the public good.

_____ 2. He has forbidden his Governors to pass Laws of immediate and pressing importance, unless suspended in their operation till his Assent should be obtained; and when so suspended, he has utterly neglected to attend to them.

_____ 3. He has refused to pass other Laws for the accommodation of large districts of people, unless those people would relinquish the right of Representation in the Legislature, a right inestimable to them and formidable to tyrants only.

_____ 4. He has called together legislative bodies at places unusual, uncomfortable, and distant from the depository of their public Records, for the sole purpose of fatiguing them into compliance with his measures.

_____ 5. He has dissolved Representative Houses repeatedly, for opposing with manly firmness his invasions on the rights of the people.

_____ 6. He has refused for a long time, after such dissolutions to, to cause others to be elected; whereby the Legislative powers, incapable of Annihilation, have returned to the People at large for their exercise; the State remaining in the meantime exposed to all the dangers of invasion from without, and convulsions within.

A. 1768, Albany County established in New York conditional to the King's stipulation that the law establishing the county make no mention of representation in New York Assembly. Colonists are outraged that new counties are without representation.

B. The Massachusetts Government Act of 1774 moved the Massachusetts legislature from Boston to Salem.

C. 1759, Governor DeLancey of New York was instructed by the King not to sign any law giving justices of the peace the authority to try minor cases unless the law contained the so-called suspending clause. The suspending clause meant that rulings were subject to the will of the King and could not be carried out until the King approved or disapproved of the matter.

D. In a rousing and emotional speech given in the Virginia Assembly, Patrick Henry offered seven resolves condemning the Stamp Act. Only the first five resolves were passed. The Royal Governor dissolved the Virginia Assembly.

E. There was general unrest in Boston. British troops had been sent into Boston to put down rioting. The Massachusetts Assembly had been dissolved. In September of 1768, a Boston town meeting called on the royal governor to convene the Assembly.

F. 1761, Upon his appointment, the Governor of New Hampshire was given instructions by the King that he could not sign any bills into law that would prohibit the importation of slaves or impose taxes or important duties on the slaves.

Name _____

C. Grievances

Read the following grievances listed, then match them to the actions taken by the king or Parliament. Which actions match which grievances?

_____ 1. He has endeavoured to prevent the population of these States; for that purpose obstructing the Laws of Naturalization of Foreigners; refusing to pass others to encourage their migrations hither, and raising the conditions of new Appropriations of Lands.

_____ 2. He has obstructed the Administration of Justice, by refusing his Assent to Laws for establishing Judiciary powers.

_____ 3. He has made Judges dependent on his Will alone, for the tenure of their offices, and the amount of payment of their salaries.

_____ 4. He has affected to render the military independent of and superior to the Civil power.

_____ 5. He has kept among us, in times of peace, standing Armies without the Consent of our legislatures.

_____ 6. For depriving us in many cases, of the benefits of Trial by Jury.

A. Various acts passed by the Parliament expanded the cases in the American colonies that could be tried in the admiralty courts. In the admiralty courts judges tried the cases not juries.

B. The Proclamation of 1763 claimed the Western lands for King George III. The Order of the council of 1773, provided that no land patents be granted without the King's assent. Parliament passed laws in 1774 that negated the existing colonial laws of naturalization. Subsequent laws made the western lands more expensive to purchase.

C. In 1768, the governor of North Carolina passed a law establishing a court system. There was a provision in the law that the British government found in contradiction to existing British law. The North Carolina Assembly would not alter the law to suit the British government. As a result, North Carolina had no court system in operation from 1773 to 1776.

D. General Thomas Gage is named Governor of Massachusetts in 1774 under a provision of the Massachusetts Government Act. He served simultaneously as head of the civil government and as commander of British forces serving in North America.

E. British law decreed that judges serve at the King's pleasure. In some cases colonial judges drew their salaries directly from the royal treasuries.

F. Great Britain sent troops to fight the French in the French and Indian War (1754-1763). The troops did not go back to Britain directly after the peace agreement was signed. The British troops were quartered in the American Colonies and the expense was paid by the colonists.

D. Grievances

Read each of the following grievances and Handout 1 (pages 6-9) and write the act or resolution by Parliament that prompted the grievance.

1. He has erected a multitude of New Offices, and sent hither swarms of Officers to harass our people, and eat out their substance. _____

_____

2. He has combined with others to subject us to a jurisdiction foreign to our constitution, and unacknowledged by our laws; giving his Assent to their Acts of pretended Legislation:

_____

3. For quartering large bodies of armed troops among us: _____

_____

4. For protecting them, by a mock Trial, from punishment for any Murders which they should commit on the Inhabitants of the States: _____

_____

5. For cutting off our Trade with all parts of the world: _____

_____

6. For imposing Taxes on us without our Consent: _____

_____

7. For transporting us beyond Seas to be tried for pretended offenses: _____

_____

8. For abolishing the free System of English Laws in neighbouring Province, establishing therein an Arbitrary government, and enlarging its Boundaries so as to render it at once an example and fit instrument for introducing the same absolute rule into these colonies.

_____

9. For taking away our Charters, abolishing our most valuable Laws, and altering fundamentally the Forms of our Governments: _____

_____

10. For suspending our own Legislatures and declaring themselves invested with power to legislate for us in all cases whatsoever. _____

_____

E. Grievances

Read the following grievances:

He has abdicated Government here, by declaring us out of his Protection and waging War against us.

He has plundered our seas, ravaged our Coasts, burnt our towns, and destroyed the lives of our people.

He is at this time transporting large Armies of foreign Mercenaries to compleat the works of death, desolation and tyranny, already begun with circumstances of Cruelty & perfidy scarcely paralleled in the most barbarous ages, and totally unworthy the Head of a civilized nation.

He has constrained our fellow Citizens taken Captive on the high Seas to bear Arms against their Country, to become the executioners of their friends and Brethren, or to fall themselves by their Hands.

He has excited domestic insurrections amongst us, and has endeavoured to bring on the inhabitants of our frontiers, the merciless Indian Savages, whose known rule of warfare, is an undistinguished destruction of all ages, sexes and conditions.

What do the grievances above have in common? Write a paragraph describing it.

_____

_____

_____

_____

_____

_____

_____

_____

_____

_____

F. The Declaration of Independence

Historians generally divide the Declaration of Independence into four parts—the statement of purpose, the contract theory of government, grievances and the conclusion. Write a brief essay including these four parts to describe the content of the Declaration of Independence.

Franklin's Cartoons

The cartoonist here, was Benjamin Franklin, considered by some, to be America's first political cartoonist. This cartoon first appeared in 1754, but was published again during the American Revolution.

Well-known symbols are often part of the political cartoonist's trade. The cartoonist relies on the reader to understand the symbols in the cartoon. One clue to understanding this cartoon is knowing that people who were superstitious at the time this cartoon was published believed that if a snake were cut up, it could come back to life again if the pieces were put back together before the sun set.

Name _____

Understanding the Cartoon

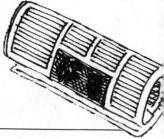

1. What does the whole snake represent? _____

2. What does each piece of the snake represent? _____

3. What does the piece of the snake that has *N.E.* written on it mean? _____

   _____

4. How does the cartoon relate to what Franklin said when he signed the Declaration of Independence? _____

   _____

   _____

5. What action does Franklin want the reader to take? _____

   _____

6. How does the cartoon relate to the superstition? _____

   _____

   _____

7. How are the colonies divided? _____

   _____

8. What is the sunset that Franklin might be talking about? _____

   _____

Beyond the Cartoon

1. Draw a cartoon that depicts the same point of view as Franklin's cartoon but with the words *United we stand, divided we fall.* Are these words as powerful as Franklin's?

   _____

   _____

2. Political cartoons employ symbolism. Symbols are used in many other aspects of our lives, too, including advertising. In what ways do advertisers use symbolism to persuade people to buy things? _____

   _____

3. On the back of this sheet, draw a political cartoon to illustrate your point of view about a current event or issue that is in the news.

Bibliography

Resources for Teachers

Bakeless, John and Katherine. *Signers of the Declaration*. Boston: Houghton Mifflin Company, 1969.

Becker, Carl. *The Declaration of Independence: A Study in the History of Political Ideas*. New York: Vintage Books, 1958.

Boyd, Julian P. *The Declaration of Independence*. Princetown, New Jersey: Princetown University Press, 1945.

Cook, Don. *The Long Fuse: How England Lost the American Colonies, 1760-1785*. New York: The Atlantic Monthly Press, 1995.

Ferris, Robert G. (Editor). *Signers of the Declaration*. Washington, D.C.: United States Department of the Interior, National Park Service, 1973.

Friedenwald, Herbert. *The Declaration of Independence: An Interpretation and an Analysis*. New York: Macmillan, 1904.

Michael, William H. *The Declaration of Independence*. Washington, D.C.: Government Printing Office, 1904.

Miller, Lillian B. *The Dye Is Now Cast*. Washington, D.C.: Published for the National Portrait Gallery by the Smithsonian Institution Press, 1975.

Sanderlin, George. *1776: Journals of American Independence*. New York: Harper & Row Publishers, 1968.

Suggested Books for Students

Lengyel, Cornel Adam. *The Declaration of Independence*. New York: Gorsset & Dunlap, 1968.

Peterson, Helen Stone. *Give Us Liberty: The Story of the Declaration of Independence*. Champaign, Illinois: Garrard Publishing Company, 1973.

Phelan, Mary Kay. *Four Days in Philadelphia*. New York: Thomas Y. Crowell Company, 1967.

Answer Key

Vocabulary Match, page 10

1. L, 2. K, 3. E, 4. N, 5. F, 6. I, 7. M, 8. C, 9. G, 10. A, 11. J, 12. B, 13. D, 14. H

Independence Scramble, page 11

1. Thomas Jefferson
2. King George III
3. Quartering Act
4. Continental Congress
5. Samuel Adams
6. George Washington
7. Richard Henry Lee
8. Lexington
9. Parliament
10. independence

Act on It–Matching, page 12

1. H, Impartial Administration of Justice Act
2. B, Sugar Act
3. D, Currency Act
4. C, Stamp Act
5. G, Revenue Act
6. F, Boston Port Act
7. A, Quartering Act
8. J, Townshend Acts
9. E, Declaratory Act
10. I, Coercive Acts

Revolutionary Time Line, page 13

1760—George III becomes king
1764—Sugar Act
1765—Stamp Act
1767—Revenue Act
1770—Boston Massacre
1773—Boston Tea Party
1774—First Continental Congress meets
1775—Battle of Lexington
1776—Declaration of Independence signed

Boston Massacre, page 14

1. Captain Thomas Preston
2. seven
3. *Butcher's Hall* is inflamatory language that paints the British as murderers.

Questions for Further Discussion, page 14

1. There was a trial, and they were found not guilty.
2. Loaded words are: *Arbitrary Power, Bloody Massacre, Perpetrated, Butcher's Hall*
3. To the colonists. To tell the American side and to inflame Americans against the British.

4. Answers will vary.

Who Were They? page 19

1. 56
2. 44
3. Benjamin Franklin, 70
4. Edward Rutledge, 26
5. English
6. roughly 70%

   English 39, 70%; Scotch-Irish 4, 7%; Scottish 3, 6%; Dutch-Scottish 2, 3%; Scottish-English 1, 2%; Swedish-English 1, 2%; Welsh-English 1, 2%; Welsh 1, 2%; Italian-English 1, 2%; Irish-Welsh 1, 2%; Irish-Dutch-English 1, 2%;

7. Lawyer:

   Lawyer 22, 40%; Merchant 10, 18%; Planter 10, 18%; Physician 4, 6%; Farmer 2, 3%; Landowner 2, 3%; Ironmaster 1, 2%; Clergyman 1, 2%; Surveyor 1, 2%; Politician 1, 2%; Judge 1, 2%; Printer 1, 2%

Questions for Further Discussion, page 19

1. Only free white men over 21 who owned property could vote. These men formed the ruling class.
2. Women could not vote until 1920.

Understanding the Declaration of Independence, page 24

A. 1. declare the reasons for independence
2. Life, Liberty and the pursuit of Happiness
3. their Creator
4. the governed
5. Governments are instituted among Men, deriving their powers from the consent of the governed.—That whenever any Form of Government becomes destructive of these ends, it is the Right of the People to alter or to abolish it, and to institute new Government, laying its foundation on such principles and organizing its powers in such form, as to them shall seem most likely to effect their Safety and Happiness.
6. The theory of the social contract is that the government and the governed have a contract. The government delivers certain services such as general defense, building highways, providing medical services and the governed support the government by paying taxes and obeying the laws.
7. to gain international approval and perhaps foreign aid from France

B. Grievances, page 25

1. F, 2. C, 3. A, 4. B, 5. D, 6. E

C. Grievances, page 26

1. B, 2. C, 3. E, 4. D, 5. F, 6. A

D. Grievances, page 27

1. Townshend Acts
2. Declaratory Act
3. Quartering Act
4. Impartial Administration of Justice Act
5. Restraining Act
6. Sugar Act, Stamp Act
7. 1769 Resolution by Parliament
8. Quebec Act
9. Massachusetts Government Act
10. Declaratory Act

E. Grievances, page 28

Answers will vary. Answers might include: All of these grievances represent actions taken by the British government that were acts of war.

F. The Declaration of Independence, page 28

Essays will vary.

Understanding the Cartoon, page 30

1. the 13 American colonies
2. individual colonies
3. New England
4. The cartoon caption "Join, or Die" directly relates to Franklin's comment, "Hang together or hang separately." It is the same message just said a different way.
5. Take up the cause against the British.
6. Even though the colonies might be defeated separately, they would be strong enough to defeat the British.
7. Each colony had a separate government, separate militia, separate charters.
8. The sunset could be the defeat of the Continental Army.

Beyond the Cartoon, page 30

1. and 2. Answers will vary.
3. Drawings will vary.

32